THE A-TEAM PRESENTS...
Top Secret Mission #1
Alex's Compromising Curse

Authored by Courtney Butorac

Illustrations by Emily Zieroth

Produced by Charity Allen

Visit www.sociallearning.org
for resources and free lesson plans
that accompany this book.

I know all the stats and all the players. I can even tell you who won the playoffs every year.

I play basketball every day at recess. When I grow up, I am going to be a basketball player.

So, on Monday, my friend Bella asked me to play kickball.

4

I said, "no, I want to play basketball." She said, "okay" and we played basketball.

5

On Tuesday, my friend Lily asked me to play four-square.

6

I said, "no, I want to play basketball." She replied, "okay" and we played basketball.

7

On Wednesday, my friend Jack asked me to play Capture The Flag.

8

I said, "no, I want to play basketball." He sighed and said, "okay" and we played basketball.

But on Friday, Max, Lily, Bella and
Jack asked me to play on the big toy.

I said, "no, I want
to play basketball."

13

"Alex," Lily replied, "we always play basketball. We want to play something else!" "But I don't want to play anything else," I said.

14

"Fine, then we aren't going to play with you." Lily said, and they walked away.

I was annoyed. Yes, it was true that they always played basketball with me but that's because it's the best game!

So, I went to shoot some hoops.

16

It wasn't as much
fun because
I was playing
all by myself.

I got bored.

That afternoon I met with my friendship group the A-Team.

We get together to learn about social skills and to help each other when we have challenges with friends or in class.

Ms. Corina, our teacher, asked if anyone had anything to talk about.

I decided to share how my friends were mean to me at recess.

19

I started to tell Ms. Corina about how nobody wanted to play basketball with me today. But, then Lily interrupted me and said that I never wanted to play anyone else's games.

Ms. Corina smiled and said, "ahhh, it sounds like you have a case of...

"For example, if Bella wanted to play soccer and Lily wanted to play baseball, they have to figure out how they can still play together and both of them be happy."

23

We moved to the carpet as Ms. Corina pulled out a poster.

"There are a number of ways to compromise, but I like to remember the big three."

"Max, can you read the first way to compromise and then give us an example?"

"Do their idea first and your idea next."

25

First Recess

Second Recess

"That means if I want to play four square and Jack wants to play tetherball, we could play tetherball at 1st recess and four square at 2nd recess," Max explained, smiling.

"Exactly!" Ms. Corina exclaimed.

26

"Lily, will you tell us the second way to compromise and give us an example?" "Mix the ideas," Lily read. "That means if I want to play castle and Bella wants to play tag we could mix the games and play CASTLE TAG!"

"Very good, Lily!" Ms. Corina said.

"Alex, do you think you could read the last one and come up with an example?"

"Choose a new idea together," I read. I thought for a second...

"So if I want to play basketball and Jack wants to play on the big toy, we could decide to play another game instead, like jump rope?"

"Yes, that is a great idea, Alex!"

"Let's practice compromising," Ms. Corina suggested.

So we acted out compromising.

Huh, I thought, compromising didn't seem so hard, and I would still get to play with my friends.

31

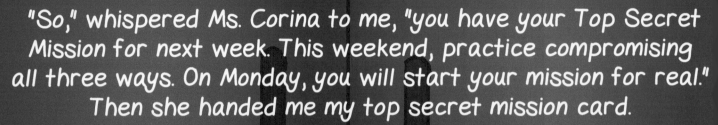

"So," whispered Ms. Corina to me, "you have your Top Secret Mission for next week. This weekend, practice compromising all three ways. On Monday, you will start your mission for real." Then she handed me my top secret mission card.

I practiced over the weekend with my mom and on Monday, I was ready to get started.

33

I waited for recess. I read my Top Secret Mission card. And when the bell rang, I ran out to the basketball court. Jack was there.

"Do you want to play basketball?" I asked him.
"Not really," he replied. "I want to play four square."

Okay, here goes, I thought. Time to compromise...

"How about we play four square at this recess, and then play basketball at the next recess?"

"Okay," Jack said. "Let's play!"

I really liked four square and I will play it again! Compromising was a good idea and it worked!

I learned how to compromise and I completed my Top Secret mission! I wonder what the next one will be...?

ABOUT THE AUTHOR

Courtney Butorac

Courtney Butorac has been supporting kids and adults with autism and also their families for 25 years as an elementary school special education teacher, preschool teacher, camp counselor and behavioral therapist. She has pioneered new ways to support social learning within her school district and is an enthusiastic member of a behavior and autism intervention team that engages district-wide to help teachers develop the knowledge and tools to support students with autism in their classrooms. Courtney has designed and facilitated powerful professional learning for educators that focuses on how to teach social skills to students with a broad range of disabilities and how to support behavioral needs in the classroom. Additionally, Courtney has guest lectured multiple times at the University of Washington's early childhood special education program.

Years ago, she and a group of her students with autism formed the A-Team friendship group to tackle the common social challenges facing her kids. These students helped inspire the "The A-Team Presents..." characters and book series.

Courtney has both a Master's Degree in early childhood special education and her Board Certification in Behavior Analysis (BCBA).

Courtney lives in Seattle with her husband, who is a fellow educator, and two young and energetic sons.

Explore more books about various social challenges in "The A-Team" book series!

Find useful, free resources on the web at sociallearning.org

THE A-TEAM PRESENTS...
Meet the A-Team
A Book About Autism

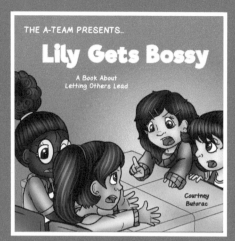

THE A-TEAM PRESENTS...
Lily Gets Bossy
A Book About Letting Others Lead

Courtney Butorac

THE A-TEAM PRESENTS...
That's Not Fair!
A Book About How Fair Isn't Always Equal

Courtney Butorac

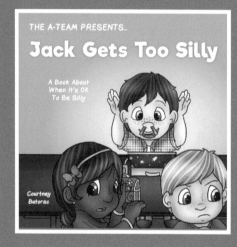

THE A-TEAM PRESENTS...
Jack Gets Too Silly
A Book About When It's OK To Be Silly

Courtney Butorac

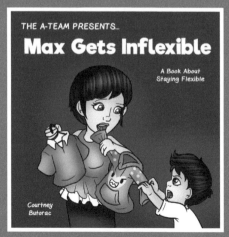

THE A-TEAM PRESENTS...
Max Gets Inflexible
A Book About Staying Flexible

Courtney Butorac

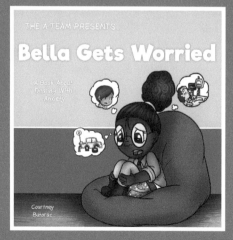

THE A-TEAM PRESENTS...
Bella Gets Worried
A Book About Dealing With Anxiety

Courtney Butorac

CPSIA information can be obtained
at www.ICGtesting.com
Printed in the USA
LVHW071029190723
752691LV00024B/93